Leaving
FATHER AND MOTHER

Leaving

FATHER *and* MOTHER

Biblical Courtship and Marriage

Cornelius Hanko

Reformed Free Publishing Association
Grandville, Michigan

© 2001 Reformed Free Publishing Association
Printed in the United States of America
All rights reserved

Originally published Dec. 1977–Aug./Sept. 1978 as a series of
articles in the *Beacon Lights*, a monthly magazine published by
the Federation of Protestant Reformed Young People's Societies.
Afterwards published as a paperback book by the Federation in
1979.

Second edition published 2001 by the Reformed Free Publishing
Association

Scripture is quoted from the Authorized (King James) Version of
the Bible

Book design by Mary Stewart (nee Hanko) and Jeff Steenholdt

Reformed Free Publishing Association
4949 Ivanrest Ave.
Grandville MI 49418-9709 U.S.A.
Phone: (616) 224-1518
Fax: (616) 224-1517
Website: www.rfpa.org
E-mail: mail@rfpa.org

ISBN: 0-916206-68-8
Library of Congress Control
  Number 2001-130167

dedicated to
the covenant young people

Contents

Preface to the First Edition

It is most heartening when covenant young people are genuinely concerned about matters of seeking a life mate, dating, and contemplating marriage.

Their deep concern and many questions occasioned my writing of the articles that appeared in *Beacon Lights*, a periodical published by the Federation of Protestant Reformed Young People's Societies.

Upon the request of parents, as well as the young people, these articles, slightly altered, now appear in a more permanent form. May the Lord bless these messages to the hearts of the youth of His church, preparing them for a blessed married life in His fear and to His glory.

REV. CORNELIUS HANKO

Chapter 1

Leaving Father and Mother

Therefore shall a man leave his father and his mother, and
shall cleave unto his wife: and they shall be one flesh.
Genesis 2:24

There comes a time in the life of the young man when he breaks away
from the parental home. After spending two decades or more in what
to him was the only home he ever knew, he forsakes that home to make
a new home for himself. This applies to the young woman also, a fact
that is so obvious that the text quoted above does not even mention it.
The young man *forsakes* father and mother. He makes a complete break
with his parents, not in the sense that he disowns them as parents, wants
nothing more to do with them, ignores them, or fails to respect them.
He still loves them, honors them, visits them, seeks their advice when
necessary, opens his home to them, and cares for them in their needs.
Yet he forsakes them so completely that their home is no longer his
home. He ventures out to establish a new home, his own home, just as
a fledgling leaves its nest, never to return, but to build its own nest
elsewhere. The young man makes a home for his bride, so that she also
packs up her belongings, moves out of her parental home, and goes to
live with her husband in their new relationship as husband and wife.

Why is that break with father and mother so complete and final?
The answer is that at the dawn of history God said that it is not good
that man should be alone. This is an ordinance of God that belongs to
man's creation. Just as a fish finds its natural habitat in the water, the
bird in the air, and the fox in the forest, so the natural environment for
the young man is in a home with his wife, requiring a break with his
former parental home.

When God created us, He created us male and female. Adam came
forth from the hand of the Creator with a strong, handsome, masculine
body. He had an intelligent face; a dexterous, multi-purpose hand; and

a keen mind. Honesty and sincerity shone from his eyes. Love to his God characterized his royal bearing. He was king; there was no doubt about that. He was king over all that he surveyed. Eve was a woman. Her long hair, her womanly figure, her feminine face: all spoke of the unique beauty of the woman. She also had a stately bearing, not that of a slave, but rather as of noble birth. Together they made a most attractive pair. In fact, it is extremely difficult for us to form a mental picture of the unblemished, radiant beauty of our first parents, who were created good, entirely fit to serve the purpose of their Maker. The inroads of sin, so evident in us, had not yet marred their natural attractiveness.

Eve was different from Adam, not only in physical appearance, but also in many other ways. She was bone of Adam's bone and flesh of his flesh, yet a new creation, formed by God to be a helper to Adam. Her love to God shone through her love and devotion to her husband. She was dependent on him to show her the marvels of creation. She admired her husband, respected him, and gladly listened to him so that she might join him in telling the praises of their Maker. They were drawn to each other, not as friends, but by the natural, magnetic attraction of the opposite sex. They were sufficiently alike, yet also sufficiently different, that they were perfectly mated. They needed each other, and that, mind you, in perfection, without sin, for sin had not yet entered to wreak havoc on that most intimate relationship between one man and one woman. It was certainly not good for man to be alone, not for Adam, nor for Eve. According to God's creation ordinance, they needed each other to make their life together complete.

There is still another reason why it was not good for Adam to be alone. God had given Adam dominion over the fish of the sea, over the fowls of the air, and over every living creature that moves upon the earth. His mandate from God was, "Be fruitful, and multiply, and replenish the earth, and subdue it." Adam was an integral part of the whole earthly creation. Paradise was his home. The vegetables that grew from the ground and the fruit that hung on the tree were at his disposal. The animals roamed the garden for his sake. Today that is very obvious to us, especially in the domestic animals: the dog, the horse, the cow, the hen. There were treasures in the earth, still unexplored, such as iron, copper, silver, gold, coal, and oil. There were the powers of electricity and of the atom still to be discovered.

There was much to do in subduing the earth. Adam could only make a small beginning in that tremendous undertaking. Therefore, he would need children to fulfill his cultural mandate. He could not remain a bachelor. He needed a mother for those children, one to bring them into this world and to help him train them for their calling in life. Only by having children, bringing into existence the human race, could he spread out and inhabit the earth to subdue it. When God said, "Be fruitful, and multiply," He even put in the man the desire to have children. A husband wants children to make his home complete. He likes to have a son of whom it is said, "He is the exact image of his father." The motherly instinct in the woman makes her yearn for a child to press to her breast, a child to claim as her very own. All this nonsense of "women's lib." is a defiant attempt to oppose God's laws, to oppose even the natural laws that are innate within the soul of every human being. The home of Adam and Eve could not be complete without children. Their lives could not be fulfilled. Their calling could not be realized. And all that was because God has said of our first parents that it was not good that they should be alone. Therefore, still today a young man leaves his father and his mother to cleave unto his wife.

A third reason why it is not good for man to be alone is that already in paradise God instituted the holy state of marriage as a picture of Christ and His church, of God and His wife. Adam was created a covenant creature to know God, to love God, and to serve God in love. He bore the very image and likeness of God in true knowledge, righteousness, and holiness. He was God's prophet, God's priest, and God's king in the midst of the earthly creation. In one word, he was God's friend-servant, living in covenant fellowship with God, walking with God, and talking with God in intimate communion life. This very covenant fellowship with God was reflected in the intimacy of Adam and Eve. Together they walked, they talked, they enjoyed each other's companionship. Eve was always ready to assist Adam in his labors in the garden. Together they experienced the love of God in their own hearts and lives. What a rich and glorious experience that was for Adam to find the same love of God echoing in Eve's heart, to have her join with him in telling the praises, the glories of their God!

They wanted children, not merely for the sake of having children, but to replenish and subdue the earth to God's glory. No other thought ever entered their minds before the fall than that they should have children who with them should fear and serve the Lord. God's ultimate purpose with them was that they should bring forth the covenant seed, the Christ, and along with Christ the whole assembly of the elect that will eternally rejoice before the throne in the new creation. If we look for the full realization of that mandate to "replenish the earth, and subdue it," we must look to Christ and to the new heavens and the new earth, where each, individually, and the whole multitude that no man can number, collectively, will bring praise and glory and honor unto our God, who created all things and works all things to that ultimate glory of the new creation. No, it was not good for Adam to be alone. How could he know the intimacy of God's covenant love in his own life? What applies to Adam applies no less to us as God's covenant people in these last days.

Ordinarily God prepares for each young man his own wife. God gives him a helper to make his life complete. In God's own time and in His own unique way, God brings as by His own hand to every man his wife. Married couples often reminisce about the strange way in which they were brought together by the providence of God. Two persons forsake father and mother and cleave (that is, are glued) to each other as one flesh. God unites two hearts, two minds, two spirits, two persons together in the unbreakable bond of marriage, which remains until "death us do part."

But more about this later. I would now like to discuss briefly the finding of a mate, the courtship, the marriage vows, and the bond of marriage that unites two lives in love, in devotion, and in the fear of the Lord.

Chapter 2

Seeking a Life Mate

There comes a time in the life of a young man that he goes out to seek a life mate for himself. This is quite natural, for when God created us, He said, "It is not good that the man should be alone; I will make him an help meet for him" (Gen. 2:18). There is nothing sinful or improper about this going out to seek a mate. This natural drive may even be spiritually motivated. A serious son of the church is not merely interested in finding a mate, but realizes that he needs a companion and a helper to carry out his calling in God's church. To fulfill his Christian stewardship he needs the comfort of his own home, the help of his wife, and the intimate love and fellowship of his family. Thus the desire to marry can be as holy as the holy institution of marriage itself.

Marriage, as we saw before, is the intimate bond of love that unites two persons and molds them together as one for life. We can think of this bond as a beautiful, variegated cord made up of three strands. We shall have occasion to refer to this in more detail later, but at this point I will only mention that the threefold strand is so tightly interwoven that it is "not quickly broken" (Eccl. 4:12).

There is, first of all, the physical, outward strand, or bond. A young man finds a certain young lady very attractive. It may be her figure, her hair, her eyes, or her dress that appeals to him. It may be her smile, the glint of her eye, or her romantic, fun-loving disposition that attracts him. This in itself is a new experience for him. Kindergarten children talk freely about the girl or the boy whom they like and intend to marry. Thereupon follows a stage when a boy would not look at a girl, much less be seen talking to her. What boy likes girls anyway? They are silly, fussy, and much more.

A girl refuses to sit next to a boy as if he is contaminated. What girl likes boys, especially if that boy happens to be her brother or the boy sitting across from her in school? If she notices him at all, she pulls up her nose. Then suddenly mother notices that her son takes a bath without being told. He is suddenly concerned about the clothing he wears. He stands in front of the mirror for a long time worrying his hair into some unnatural position. Or else it is the daughter who wants to wear her best clothing to an outing, takes a month's supply of clothing along for a four-day convention, and runs the comb through her long locks at every opportunity. Father and mother wisely look the other way, but both now realize why John does not hear when he is spoken to, and why Mary has that faraway look.

There is also a second strand of the threefold cord: the psychological attraction of the sexes. Mary is a kind, sweet girl. She is a lot of fun. She also plays the piano well. John may have known her for years, may have lived almost next door to her and attended the same school with her. Now suddenly he realizes that she is alive, even though in times past he was as blind as a bat to her pleasant smiles intended only for him. Mary, on her part, likes John. He is a brain. He is also good at sports. And he has nice hair. Shakespeare said that "Love is blind, and lovers cannot see the pretty follies that themselves commit." I tend to think that when it comes to looking each other over and sizing each other up, both sexes have their eyes wide open. It has been said that people should keep both eyes wide open before marriage and would do well to keep one closed after marriage. There is wisdom in that. In this connection it should be said that opposites attract. God in His wisdom brings two persons together who will serve perfectly as a balance wheel for each other. The one may be impetuous: speaking, acting before he thinks. The other may weigh her words and actions carefully. Imagine what would happen if they were both alike! The one may tend to be pessimistic; the other can see the rainbow in the cloud. One may be an introvert; the other may carry her heart on her coat sleeve. The one may tend to be miserly; the other may be too extravagant. Subconsciously the one is drawn to the other as by magnetic attraction to fill in the lack in his or her own life.

The marriages in the world consist of just two strands, the physical and psychological. Even in that respect, man is usually a poor judge of himself as well as a poor judge of others, readily influenced by outward, sexual appeal. The result is that though from a natural and a legal point of view these are real marriages, they still are only caricatures of the genuine, holy marital union. The important spiritual strand is missing. The strongest tie of all is lacking, so that the other two are readily strained to a breaking point.

The spiritual strand is the third bond, and it unites two people *in the Lord*. The Lord brings them together in His favor. The love of Christ in our hearts draws us to those who love the Lord. A Christian young man seeks his companion in the church, simply from the principle, "Thy people shall be my people, and thy God my God" (Ruth 1:16). Even though his sinful flesh may be drawn for a moment to outward appearance and the vivacious lure of an unbeliever, his heart tells him that this is no good; it is sinful in the sight of God. A sincere believer is a companion of those who seek the Lord, and his heart tells him, "Do not I hate them, O LORD, that hate thee? . . . I hate them with perfect hatred: I count them mine enemies" (Ps. 139: 21, 22). One who loves the Lord avoids anyone who takes God's Name in vain or uses foul language. He loathes the mad, lustful music, the movies, and the dances relished by sinners. Anyone who takes his faith seriously cannot condone defiance of those in authority, endangering one's life by reckless driving, or experimenting with liquor, drugs, gambling, or the like. The child of God is drawn to one who speaks his language in spiritual matters, who enjoys with him the things of God's kingdom. This spiritual bond proves to be the sustaining, molding power in a couple's married life, the gyroscope of their ship in stormy seas, the compass that keeps them on a straight course to the Haven of Rest.

Seeking a life mate is a serious matter. Young men should not play the field to see how many scalps they can collect in their belts before they settle down. The young woman should not play the field to see how many fellows will fall victim to her charm, how many shattered hearts and broken hopes she can leave along her trail before she marries. Dating is not a frivolous game that can be played without doing serious damage to some innocent victim. It has happened many times that after an unfortunate love affair, a young man grabbed the first girl he could get, or the young woman threw herself at some undesirable person, perhaps just for spite, maybe in desperation. The outcome was a very unhappy marriage. Who is the culprit who should carry the blame? Human emotions are not playthings. Making love is not a sport. One may well remember the golden rule: "Do unto others as you would have them do unto you." There is nothing worse for a young person than to be "stood up," or plainly, to have been made the fool.

I do think that a young man may ask a girl for a casual date for the purpose of making better acquaintance. Young people in high school, especially, should not take their dating too seriously. They have plenty of time for that in the future. They should also remember that they are undergoing a tremendous physical and psychological change, as well as spiritual growth. More advanced education often changes a person's outlook on life, and along with that, the idea of a life mate. A high school sweetheart may not prove to be a fit wife or husband, or even a fit parent for the children. There are married folk who will tell you that they never dated another boy or girl friend, but "went together" already in junior high and in high school and still are perfectly happy. That is possible, but young people must be sure that they are meant for each other before they become serious in their courtship. Marriage must be the goal in dating, even though this is not discussed on the first date, and even though one is only seeking to become better acquainted.

The question could arise, Who should make the approach? Should the girl ask the fellow, or should she wait until she is asked? It may sound a bit old fogyish in a day of women's lib., yet I still think that it is the prerogative of the boy to ask the girl. A girl should not appear to be too aggressive. This does not mean that she sits quietly at home waiting for a phone call for her first date. If my observations do not deceive me, most girls have the natural ability to attract the attention of the young man who interests them. A girl does not throw herself at a man, nor does she use foul tactics to win him, as if anything is fair in love or war. Still, her winsome ways and pleasant smile can do much to attract a boy's attention.

One final remark in this connection: do not neglect to pray. Scripture says that we must make all our needs known to God in heaven. Desiring a life mate is an essential need. Pray about it. Pray much. Pray that God may direct you to the mate of His choice to insure a happy marriage. In olden times, the father sought out a mate for his son or his daughter. Young people had to be content with the arrangements that the parents made. You would not like that, would you? Yet be sure to read the scriptural account of Abraham's servant going to Haran to find a wife for Isaac. Realizing that this undertaking was much too big for him to handle, he committed the whole matter to the Lord. His answer came sooner than he expected. No one could be more certain than Isaac that he had received a wife from the Lord, and that as answer to prayer.

Chapter 3

Courtship

Tennyson wrote, "In the spring a young man's fancy lightly turns to thoughts of love." There may be something to that, but I doubt very much that this particular fancy is limited to one season of the year. Whether this be in the season when flowers begin to bloom and the birds seek their mates, or at any other time of the year, a young man and a young lady should take the matter of courtship seriously.

I spoke before of the young man and his girl friend going out together to become better acquainted. Getting acquainted is more important than we often realize. To one who has fallen frantically in love, it may seem strange that he does not know his girl friend. The very thought of her brings stars to his eyes, while she sits mooning over her schoolwork as if she were miles away. Not know each other? Listen. There are many young people who plunge into marriage only to realize that they have never learned to know each other. Living together in the most intimate relationship of husband and wife is far different from living with your brothers and sisters, far different from associating with your friends and schoolmates. Seeing one another across the breakfast table in the morning and greeting each other after a harried day's work is quite different from the formal meetings before marriage when you are dressed in your Sunday best and on your best behavior. More than one married person has thought, and maybe even said, "My father married my mother, but I married a stranger." It would be nice if these polite formalities, these kind words, these little gifts that make your day before you are married, could also be continued after married life has become a daily routine. Getting to know each other, even down to personal idiosyncrasies, is most essential for a happy future. Marriage is for life; rushing into it threatens nothing less than total disaster.

Therefore, for a good courtship, Rule 1 is, *Get to know each other.*

This is all-important. I have had young people, after a hasty, exciting romance, come to me to talk about wedding plans. When I asked them about their differences, their different backgrounds, different family ties, and different church connections, my questions were brusquely brushed aside with the curt answer, "We're in love." Who, after all, can challenge such a powerful, all-sufficient power as "love"? If you were to suggest that this "love" appears to be nothing more than heated passion, and that this "love" is not everything that it is set up to be, you would be branded as a dried-up, old fogy, who doesn't really know what the word "love" is all about. If you would make bold to suggest that these young folks should let their love experience cool a bit before they dash headlong into marriage, you would be frowned upon in total disgust. My experience has been that these same people, a few bitter and disillusioning years later, were ready to admit that they made a bad mistake. They reached the conclusion that they were not meant for each other at all, yet unless they learn to love each other in the Lord, they are compelled to live with their mistake the rest of their lives.

Get to know each other. You cannot attain that by going out for a ride, spending long hours under the moonlight at some lonely spot, embracing and making love far into the night. The "now" generation may not like to hear this, but it is still a sound rule that no good ever came from being together after midnight. Parents should insist, and I mean insist, that their fledgling be home before or at midnight, or be able to give a good reason for staying out later. One could sincerely wish that all parents who love their children would agree to demand that they obey a curfew. So often young folks fear the scorn and the sneers of others who are allowed to come in when they please. Too often parents are afraid that their children will lack popularity if they are too strict about a curfew. Is the approval of others or is popularity the price you want to pay for a seared conscience, a condoning of sin, or even irreparable damage to soul and body and to your future? You will never get to know each other by watching movies, enjoying a late late show, experimenting with dancing, or indulging in smutty novels, filthy magazines, pornography, or anything of the sort, whether you do that singly or together. You can never learn to know each other, either, by sitting together whispering sweet nothings in each other's ears or trying to show with your actions how much you care.

If you want to know each other, you must discuss subjects of common interest. It is a bad sign if you cannot find plenty of topics that you enjoy talking about together. If you have no common interests before you are married, do you expect to find them afterward? Another question arises: Are your common interests worthwhile? Will they make for a life of friendship and fellowship together? John must be able to say, "I can't wait to talk to Mary about this. She and I understand each other; we like to talk about the same things." Mary should say, "This I have to talk over with John," or "This program, this book, this entertainment is as valuable to John as it is to me."

Above all, you simply must agree on your doctrinal and spiritual convictions. Nothing cuts deeper than a spiritual breach between two persons. Nothing is worse than a realm of "I must not talk about that," especially when this deals with what is most precious to you: your faith. I do not say that you must always agree on everything you talk about. A little spat or a warm argument occasionally is refreshing and enriching. However, you must be of the same doctrinal and religious convictions. That is simply a *must.* If you contemplate being joined at some future date in the permanent bond of marriage, you must be of one heart and one mind when it comes to your spiritual life. There may be so many things that you like about your boyfriend, or about your girl friend, that seem so all-important at the moment that the fact that you go to different churches, that you have an entirely different religious background, seems unimportant. Again, you may be inclined to say, "We have so much in common, how can that religious difference ever stand as a barrier between us or interfere with our happiness?" Never try to convince yourselves that time is bound to obliterate any religious differences between you. Get them settled *now.* Too often emotions have taken over before these things were settled. If you agree doctrinally, and are both spiritually minded in your outlook on life, you already have a sound basis for a happy marriage. Common interests, along with differences in makeup, make you long to see and talk to each other.

Rule 2 is, *Get to know each other's family.*

It is true, of course, that you are marrying the boy or the girl, and not the family, but the fact remains that you are marrying *into* the family. Besides, your prospective life mate comes from that family, has lived with that family for some twenty years, and will remain an integral part of that family. Is the fear of the Lord in that home? Is there a Christian attitude among the members of the family? Is there a Christian atmosphere in the home? If not, you will have to make doubly sure that your friend is of such sturdy spiritual caliber that he or she can stand alone and maintain strong religious principles throughout your life together, even in opposition to the home that opposes these principles. If your friend's family is a Christian family, make sure that there are no serious differences on doctrine, on godly walk, on world-and-life-view. You are safest when you marry within the Protestant Reformed denomination, that is, if you marry a sincere believer within the denomination.

Too often a young man ignores Christian principles, brushing them aside with the confident air that all problems will be straightened out after marriage. Too often the young woman will pride herself with the notion that she can reform her husband after they are settled down and undo what home influence did to him for twenty years. (Is it the mother instinct in her to believe this?) The young man may well watch his girl friend's mother. What kind of wife is she to her husband? How does she treat her children? Is that the kind of wife, mother, cook, housekeeper, and companion he is looking for in the daughter? If not, is he sure that the daughter does not take after her mother in this respect? The traditional picture of the mother-in-law is that of an interfering, miserable person. Don't put too much stock in that. There are many very considerate, kind, helpful mothers-in-law who are appreciated for what they are. When the young lady goes to her friend's home to make acquaintance with the family, she may well take a good look at her prospective father-in-law. Is he a husband who shows genuine concern for his wife, or is he the self-centered individual who thinks that the whole world should revolve around him? Is he a father who is interested in his children? Does he have time for his family, or does he stow himself away behind the newspaper or in front of the television? Maybe your boyfriend does not take after his father. Perhaps he has his mother's nature, but it is well to be sure before you become too deeply involved.

Rule 3 is, *Take time to enjoy your courtship without hastily plunging into marriage.*

Do not marry too young. I leave it to you to determine just exactly how young is *too* young. Some young people mature sooner than others. Be sure that you are not too young when you take on the grave responsibilities that are involved in married life. The mature teen years are the happiest, most carefree time of life. Enjoy them; make the most of them because they never return.

Plan for your marriage carefully. Make the most of a pleasant, useful courtship, preparing yourselves for the biggest venture you will ever undertake in your life, the venture of holy matrimony. Boys who marry too young find themselves cut off from all the fun that other young people of their age are having. There are two mouths to feed, a home that must be kept up, burdens that are far too great for young shoulders to bear. Young girls may soon find themselves pregnant, with a fear that drives them in desperation into mother's arms, saying, "I never knew it would be like this!" Young fathers often treat their first baby like a toy, something to be played with and then abruptly put aside. Young mothers regard their little ones like dolls and seem helpless in handling them as real people. I have often marveled that a babe survived as well as it did. No, do not rush into marriage. Sage advice is not to see each other too often, especially not every night, not until the final plans for the wedding are being made. Prepare for your marriage with a level head and a praying heart that is attuned to God and to His Word. Prepare yourselves for the future, not only by buying furniture and silverware, but also by prayerfully seeking that two hearts may truly become one in the Lord.

Rule 4 is, *Build up a strong esteem for each other, keeping for yourselves a good conscience.*

Negatively, do not let your sexual impulses get out of hand. A young man may entice his girl friend to see how far she will let him go in giving vent to his sexual urge. A young woman may be afraid of losing her boyfriend if she acts too coy, too cold, too prudish in matters of sex. Besides, scant clothing, short skirts, open blouses, trips to the beach, close physical contact with each other, and many other factors arouse the passions to the extent that they readily get out of control. Solomon speaks of a dumb animal that allows itself to be led to the slaughter. Carnal lusts can cast all reason to the wind, with the result that sin breeds sin, one evil step leads to another, and a good courtship is ruined, even though every effort is put forth to prevent pregnancy. Still worse, both are troubled with a bad conscience. The urge to see each other is filled with strong passions and horrible apprehensions. One tends to blame the other, while mutual self-respect and self-esteem have disappeared. Most of the problems that arise after marriage stem from the passionate courtship before marriage. Husband and wife soon realize that what they mistook for love was nothing but sinful lust. When that desire is satisfied, their marriage is threatened with disaster. No sound marriage can be built on anything as flimsy as physical attraction. The only solution, even at that late date, is that they meet at the cross, confess their sins, seek forgiveness of God and of each other, and find a sound spiritual basis for their marriage in the Lord. Sad to say, this is a rather late date to discover this.

Positively, build up a strong esteem for each other. Be spiritually minded in your courtship. We must not hold a double standard of morality, as if liberties are allowed to lovers that are not allowed to other single persons and to the married. The commandment "Thou shalt not commit adultery," with all its implications, applies as much to single as to married persons. Love one another, not only as boy and girl, but also as you are drawn to each other by the magnetism of your different personalities, and above all by your love and devotion to your God. As a young man, do not become the Tempter's tool to the one you love. Love her so much that you want to admire her for what she is. Preserve her purity for herself and for you. As a young woman, do not lure with sexual appeal, suggestive words, and actions. If you love your boyfriend, keep his conscience pure before God. Admire him for his moral strength and convictions. If you plan to wear a white gown on that long-dreamed-of wedding day, be sure that your gown reflects the truth that you come to your husband as a virgin, a picture of Christ's bride, and not as a possible cast-off, second-hand, polluted maid. Build up esteem for one another before your marriage so that afterward you may, as husband, love and cherish your wife as your very own possession; and as wife, respect your husband as worthy of your trust throughout the years to come. Pray. Pray constantly: "Lead us not into temptation, but deliver us from evil." With all the emphasis on sex in magazines, books, on television, and everywhere else, it cannot be stressed too strongly that young people in their courtship must keep themselves unspotted from the world. God blesses a pure courtship with the assurance that He preserves us from evil and will bless us also when we venture out upon life's sea in the ship of holy matrimony.

Chapter 4

Single Persons
Who Do Not Marry

In our discussion, we may not ignore those who never leave father and mother to enter the marriage state. Therefore, we devote this chapter to those who remain single all their lives, not because they need commiseration, but because I am convinced that they also have a special place and calling in God's church.

As we may expect, Scripture gives us guidelines in regard to single persons. Paul speaks rather extensively about them in I Corinthians 7. Evidently the church at Corinth had written Paul about certain problems in the church. Among these was the question whether it was proper that single people remained in the single state. Paul proceeds to answer the question, immediately impressing upon the congregation at Corinth that there is nothing wrong with a person remaining single. He even declares that it is good and morally excellent for a man not to touch a woman, that is, to remain unmarried. Although it is the general rule in the world, and also in the church, that a man or woman marries, this does not mean that it is obligatory. In verse 7 of this chapter, Paul states that he would that all men were even as himself, that is, unmarried. He repeats in verse 26 that it is good for a man (or woman) to remain single, and he adds in verse 27, "Art thou bound unto a wife? seek not to be loosed. Art thou loosed from a wife? seek not a wife." At the conclusion of the chapter, he mentions that a woman is happier if she does not marry.

At first glance, these passages from I Corinthians seem to be in conflict with the rest of the Scriptures. Paul states in I Corinthians 7:1, "It is good for a man not to touch a woman." Genesis 2:18 teaches us, "It is not good that the man should be alone."

The contradiction is, however, more imaginary than real. If Paul were to advocate celibacy, or to teach that a single life is holier or more pleasing to God than married life, he would be in conflict with the Scriptures and with his own writings. The apostle always maintains that "marriage is honourable in all, and the bed undefiled" (as taught in Heb. 13:4). Paul presents the marriage of believers as a picture of Christ and His church (Eph. 5:32). However, Paul does say that there are definite advantages for those who do not enter the marriage state. Married persons are liable to involve themselves so much in their families that the kingdom of heaven does not receive its due. Paul also saw days of persecution approaching for the church at Corinth, so that those who were not bound by marriage should not involve themselves lest the burden of persecution be made heavier by the duties of a family. The apostle speaks of being happier in the single state, primarily with single-minded dedication toward the kingdom of heaven in mind, not denigrating the role of marriage as a covenant responsibility.

Scripture considers the role of the single person in the church unique and vital. Let us consider the instruction Jesus gives us in Matthew 19:12, where He says,

> For there are some eunuchs, which were so born from their mother's womb: and there are some eunuchs, which were made eunuchs of men: and there be eunuchs, which have made themselves eunuchs for the kingdom of heaven's sake. He that is able to receive it, let him receive it.

A eunuch, according to the definition in the dictionary, is a castrated male. This may be taken literally, referring to someone who was self-mutilated. Kings in the old dispensation would sometimes make their servants eunuchs to prevent any problems with their sexual drive. This was especially true in the case of officers in the army or with chamberlains who worked in the harems. The word "eunuch," therefore, can refer to a servant or slave in the general sense of the word, or can also refer to a chamberlain. The law of Moses forbad anyone who was thus mutilated to serve in the temple (Lev. 21:16ff.) or even to attend the public worship (Deut. 23:1). The very idea of such emasculation was completely abominable to God and to true Israel. In Jesus' day, eunuchs were still known, even as we read of the Ethiopian eunuch in the book of Acts. There are those who have such complete mastery of their sexual desires that they are not interested in marriage for themselves.

Jesus mentions three possibilities. There are eunuchs who are born with a natural restraint to sexual impulses. There are also those eunuchs who are forced to remain single by the attendant circumstances of life or who choose to remain as single persons for their own personal reasons. Finally, there are eunuchs for the sake of the kingdom of heaven. I want to say a few words about each of these.

We are all aware of the fact that there are people who, because of some physical handicap or some other reason, simply cannot marry. They may be born with the natural gift of continence, the sexual urge in them never being very strong. Evidently God does not intend that these should marry. They certainly should not marry for ulterior motives.

In a woman, the ulterior desire to marry may be triggered by a desire to have a home of her own, to have someone support her, or to have a male companion, to name but a few. If, for example, a woman hates housework, hates to be bothered with children hanging on her skirts, hates the cares and worries of a family, but on the other hand, likes to have her own career and likes to live her own life, that woman should not marry under any circumstance. She should make up her mind that she was brought into this world not to marry, but to use her gifts and talents in some other way.

This holds true for a man also. In a man, the ulterior desire to marry may be triggered by the need to have a home, to fit in with his friends, or to be cared for by a woman. Yet he, too, may be totally unsuited for the rigors of marriage and family. A man may not be suited for the nurture of children and may not be able to become family-oriented. He should give prayerful consideration to the use of his talents in another way and should not marry simply to follow the crowd. Those who marry for ulterior motives, and not because they are suited for marriage, can only make life miserable for themselves, for their mates, and for the children they may receive.

Jesus speaks of a second group, who either through attendant circumstances, or by their own choice, do not marry. There was a time when anything related to sex was considered filthy, whether among the single or the married. People thought that the only reason the Bible gives for marriage is to prevent fornication (see, for example, I Cor. 7:2). They never read that "marriage is honourable in all, and the bed undefiled" (Heb. 13:4). Nor did they understand that Scripture speaks of a *holy* marriage state. They spoke behind their hands about married people, hid themselves with shame when they were pregnant, and often with a false sense of decency would avoid discussing sex openly with anyone, unless they did so in a contemptuous manner. These people, if they did marry, often made their marriages most unhappy because of their perverted view of the holy institution that God Himself introduced into our lives in the state of righteousness in paradise.

There are young men, and likely also young women, who for their own selfish reasons either never marry or postpone marriage as long as possible. Often these single persons have a good job, make good money, and enjoy spending their time and money on sports and pleasures for their selfish interests. They can afford to buy themselves a nice car, go on vacations, indulge in all kinds of luxuries, and live a carefree life of self-indulgence. They look with a bit of disgust upon their former friends who are struggling to support a family, who walk the floor at night with a baby on their arm, and who appear to be most miserable with a ball and chain that keeps them home. These single folk should remember that they are wasting important years of their lives, stealing the time and talents God has entrusted to them for their selfish ambitions, while they should be devoting themselves as good stewards in God's house to the things of God's kingdom. Too often they forget, or ignore, their covenant obligation. Unless they are celibate to the glory of God to function better for His kingdom, they are covenantally bound to marry and give birth to the church of God. Too often this covenant duty is forgotten, not prayerfully considered, buried under selfish desires. Let these young men and women bear in mind that in the great day of days they must give account of what they have done with these important years of their lives when they should have been preparing themselves for more useful duties in God's church.

Young people who put off marriage because they are enjoying themselves too much in their carefree way of life are also a bad example for younger brothers and sisters, as well as for younger members of the church. You can see young boys looking with green-eyed envy and admiration at the brand-new sports car or the new boat of the single fellow. You can recognize the yearning of young girls first to have their fling before they settle down to the serious business of speaking their marriage vows and the humdrum of married life.

Worse, some of these young men, instead of living like bachelors, enjoy taking out girls without becoming too "serious" with them. It seems to appeal to them to have a different girl for each occasion. No doubt, this often becomes more than just an evening out. These young men may even expect from each girl a certain amount of necking, whispers of affection, or more, while they are only interested in "a good time" and little concerned about what they may be doing to the girl.

There are girls also who use men merely to flatter their pride and to satisfy their carnal desires. These people are definitely hurting themselves as well as others. Peter speaks of carnal lusts "which war against the soul" (I Peter 2:11). These carnal lusts are like a host of demons that make their assault upon the soul, depriving us of spiritual sensitivity, forcing our consciences into silence, drawing us ever further into the snares and allurements of sin. Reason flies out of the window; wild passion has its fling. Many an innocent victim who took the advances seriously discovers too late that he or she was but a pawn, to be thrown away like an old shoe when the fun was over. Many a heart has been broken, many a life irreparably damaged by the flighty fancy of these thoughtless, selfish young people. Remember, as brothers and sisters in Christ, we are bound before God to care for and nurture one another, both spiritually and physically. When we treat one another in such a careless way, we are an abomination to the Lord.

A word of warning fits in here quite nicely. There are some boys, but there are particularly girls, who are so haunted by the specter of remaining single that they will throw themselves at most anyone who is available. Later, some of them will make no secret that they regret the day that they plunged into marriage to escape being branded an old maid or a bachelor. Marriage is so permanent. A lifetime is a long time to grieve with a wrong mate. Married life at best has its problems. Our Marriage Form begins with the statement that "married persons are generally, by reason of sin, subject to many troubles and afflictions."[1] That is so much worse in a marriage where the partners are not suitably mated. What fools people can be to deliberately rush into a lifelong misery to avoid being unwanted or thought undesirable!

I don't know why, but in all the years of my ministry I have seen attractive, intelligent girls (and boys) passed by within the church only because the grass looked greener on the other side. As some of the young men once said to me, "We can't marry the girls in our own church. We know them too well. They're like sisters." Yet some of them did marry within their own church, and they were happy as a result of it. The point I want to make is this, young men and young women: Don't ruin your lives by plunging into an unhappy marriage. And especially, do not marry outside the church. If you begin marriage as truly one in the Lord, any difficulties ahead are manageable. Do not risk the joy, the serenity of the church of God, merely for a band of gold. There are worse things than remaining single all your life.

There is still a third group, of whom Christ says that they have made themselves eunuchs for the sake of the kingdom of heaven. This should not be taken in the literal sense, as if Jesus were to advocate self-mutilation. There is a more excellent way for the sincere child of God to suppress and gain mastery over his sexual desires. All may not be able to attain this; let them marry. But it is possible for men and women to control their natural instincts as if they were sexless. The victory they attain by their self-restraint is far more valuable to them than a negative, feelingless situation created by emasculation. Jesus speaks of making themselves eunuchs for the kingdom of heaven. They become so absorbed in their work that they have neither the time nor the desire to give themselves to marriage. Jesus Himself was a perfect picture of becoming so engrossed in the work entrusted to Him that in the closing

---

1. The Form for the Confirmation of Marriage Before the Church is found in *The Psalter: With Doctrinal Standards, Liturgy, Church Order, and Added Chorale Section.* Rev. ed., PRC. (Grand Rapids, Mich.: William B. Eerdmans Publishing Company, 1998), 115.

hours of His life He could say, "I have glorified thee on the earth: I have finished the work which thou gavest me to do" (John 17:4). Elijah in the old dispensation, and Paul in the new, are examples of complete devotion to the things of God's kingdom, so that these men had no desire to marry. In I Corinthians 9:5, Paul states that he had as much right to have a wife as any of the other apostles, yet that evidently was not his desire.

This peculiar position of remaining single for the sake of the kingdom of heaven may not have been a matter of choice with some men and women. Many single persons, particularly women, simply did not have the opportunity to get married when they were young. Even though they would gladly have had a boyfriend, for some reason or another this privilege never came to them. They may even have prayed that the Lord would lead them to a life mate of His choosing, only to discover that the Lord had not planned a mate for them. Rather than becoming bitter or sour on life, these young women sought to use their gifts and talents in the church. We are thankful for them, especially for those who have become devoted teachers of our covenant children. They will undoubtedly realize, especially when they stand before the great white throne, that they served God's cause and kingdom better this way than in any other.

Often the unmarried men and women feel left out. They are too old to associate with the young people of the church. They cannot join the Mr. and Mrs. Societies. They are not invited to affairs involving married couples. In fact, they often feel themselves looked down on by the married people, as if they belong to the unwanted. This is not right and is an injustice that the married do well to avoid. We must all see the providence of God in keeping some people single. God has His own purpose with each of us. He knows how we can best use our life, our health and strength, and our gifts and talents to His glory. For each one of us is God's workmanship, God's carefully formed masterpiece, created in Christ Jesus unto those good works which God has before ordained that we should walk in them. By all means let all of our single saints be thankful to the Lord for His benefits, living a full and rich life in the fear of the Lord. Let them use their time and effort, their gifts and talents that God has entrusted to them, in a most useful manner in God's church. There are so many things that need to be done, but there is so little time to do them, and qualified persons are often hard to find. God has given you your unique place in His church and kingdom. He has also a work for you to perform as only you can perform it. If you fail to find your specific task, ask the Lord to show you, and follow His leading.

Chapter 5

Engagement

John and Mary are engaged. They have been going steady for some time, have developed a growing appreciation and love for each other, have prayed that the Lord would make plain to them whether they were meant for each other, and have settled whatever differences there were between them in regard to their religious principles, church membership, and the like. John is elated at the thought that Mary has consented to become his wife. Mary is almost beside herself with joy as she displays proudly the ring that John gave her to seal their engagement. We share their joy on this wonderful occasion.

These two young people now enter into an entirely new phase of their lives. Their betrothal, or engagement, is, after all, a very serious matter. If one turns to Scripture, he finds that a betrothal had its own spiritual implications. The betrothal, as such, consisted of three acts.

First, a contract was drawn up by the parents or by the friend of the bridegroom. There is no evidence that the prospective bride had any say in the matter. Think, for example, of Abraham, who sent his servant to Haran to obtain a wife for Isaac. We cannot help but admire this servant for his faith and humble trust in God. The mission he was sent out to accomplish was too big for him to handle, so he committed it into the hands of the Almighty. There is a lesson here for us.

Second, the two families often met together to discuss the terms of the contract. In the case of Jacob and Leah, this was rather a one-sided deal. Laban had all the advantage and made the most of it, hiring Jacob for seven years to earn his daughter, and then by deceit, obtaining seven more years of service from his son-in-law. But the idea of a contract or agreement between the two families was common procedure.

Third, there was payment of the dowry (see Gen. 34:12, Ex. 22:17). The money payment belonged at first to the family, but later the bride shared one-third. Before the marriage proper, the bride-to-be stayed in the home of her parents. In the case of a virgin, one year elapsed before the wedding; in the case of a widow, at least thirty days. The prospective bridegroom and bride were considered virtually married so that if either party wanted the engagement broken, divorce proceedings would have to be sought. This is evident from the incident of Joseph and Mary. Joseph could publicly have exposed Mary as a woman unfaithful to her vow, yet he was so reluctant to question her purity that he preferred to put her away quietly.

We should notice that Scripture makes betrothal a picture of God taking His church, or His people, unto Himself. This is beautifully expressed in Ezekiel 16:8:

> Now when I passed by thee, and looked upon thee, behold, thy time was the time of love; and I spread my skirt over thee, and covered thy nakedness: yea, I sware unto thee, and entered into a covenant with thee, saith the Lord GOD, and thou becamest mine.

For Israel as a nation, this referred to the time when God looked at their affliction in Egypt, delivered them with a mighty hand, and established His covenant with them at Sinai. That, in turn, is a picture of our spiritual deliverance from the forlorn nakedness of our sins into the redeeming grace of Christ, to be taken into intimate fellowship with our God forever. Also in this spiritual sense, our betrothal to God is inseparably bound up with the eternal marriage of Christ and His bride. As far as the figure, "and I spread my skirt over thee" is concerned, we find the same figure in Ruth 3:9, where it refers to Ruth's request that Boaz take her to wife.

All that has been said points to the binding power of an engagement. The word "betrothal" means literally, "To pledge one's troth, or faithfulness, to another person." The same idea underlies the word "engagement," which means, "To bind or bring under a pledge, as by oath, pledge, contract or promise."

The formality of an engagement has almost disappeared entirely. Not so many years ago, a suitor would have an understanding with his girl friend but would not actually become her fiancé without first consulting his parents and then making a formal call on his girl friend's parents to gain their permission to marry their daughter. Only after this consent was granted would she receive a ring. Much of this takes place informally today. No doubt, the couple do seek advice of their parents, or at least their tacit approval, and then the young man takes his girl out to dinner and presents her with a ring. The parents are informed of the engagement later. There is one danger in our present practice, and that is that we lose sight of the fact that an engagement is a vow of fidelity, as well as a promise to marry. There was a time, not even in the hoary past, when breaking an engagement was considered such a serious matter that, unless good reasons could be produced, the responsible party was held guilty before the church of breach of promise, a sin against the third commandment. Although this is not practiced today, we must, nevertheless, remember that a promise is a promise, an oath is an oath, and a vow is a vow, none of which may be carelessly broken.

Now the time has arrived for closer intimacy. Before the engagement, both parties dressed, as it were, in their Sunday best. Each had put on the very best front in order to please the other, or to win the other. That time is past. Both recognize the other as more than a dear friend; they are prospective life mates. If any differences of a serious nature remain, they should be cleared up at once. It is to be expected that there will be sharp differences of opinion, or likes and dislikes, of background or habits, which become more evident now than in the past. Two different lives do not readily mold into one, not even in marriage. These differences usually prove interesting and pose no serious problem. God in His wisdom brings together two people who are sufficiently alike, yet also sufficiently different, that they complement each other, forming one whole, forming a balance wheel for each other as well.

There may, however, appear serious character faults that prove not to be correctable. A prospective husband may show certain ambitions, aims in life that are contrary to a Christian walk, and he may refuse to give up these ambitions. The young man may have a drinking habit, or a drug habit, or may be enslaved to foul and profane language. A girl may reveal that she abhors housework, dislikes children, and has her own selfish ambitions for the future. She may be domineering, determined to "rule the roost." The young man may be ever so handsome and warm in his affections, the envy of all the girls around; the girl may be very attractive and appealing; but the time has come to face reality—the inward person—prayerfully and sincerely. The young man must not think that a trip to the altar is going to make a radical change in his fiancé. The motherly instinct in the woman must not give her the notion that her kindness and understanding can reform the man she sees in her future. My personal comment at this point would be that I have seen weddings that were much more painful to me than a funeral service. I would rather have brought one or the other to the grave than witness them taking a step that was bound to lead to disaster. My warnings all too often proved well-grounded. It is better to agree to break an engagement than to continue together in what obviously can only be a sinful walk, which can never carry the approval of the Lord. There is one time when an oath is not binding, and that is when we would sin against our God by carrying it out. Remember, love is not as blind as it is put up to be, and pure sentiment must not determine your future.

This raises the subject of compatibility, about which much has been written in recent times. Various tests are improvised, discussion groups organized, visits to psychologists are scheduled—all in order to be certain that the two persons contemplating marriage are properly suited for each other and to counsel them accordingly. The reason for this concern about compatibility must arise from the ever increasing number of divorces, as well as from the many marital problems that vex and disrupt families.

Some persons are so reluctant to bind themselves in marriage that they prefer to live together without the formality of a marriage license. Others would like to marry on a contract basis, binding themselves for only a limited time, to be free to separate if their relationship proves wearisome or unsuccessful. There is no doubt about it that the rapid degeneration of the human race is making its inroads into marriage relationships. In the past, there were also those who did not get along as husband and wife, some of whom sought a divorce, but the majority of whom bore up with a bad situation. The world frowned upon breaking up a home, and the church considered this a censurable sin. Times have changed, however. Today separation and divorce have become so widespread that even the churches sympathize with a divorced person, considering that a divorce is a lesser sin than living together in disharmony. The hope is always cherished that the next venture may prove more successful.

As covenant young people contemplating marriage, you should not allow these tragic experiences to fill your souls with fear. You have a security that the world does not have, that no one has who dashes headlong into marriage with no greater idea than sexual satisfaction. First, you have the love of God in your hearts, which is the basic bond of unity between you. Second, you have prayerfully committed your way to the Lord, so that you became engaged in the assurance that God brought you together in His goodness. (By the way, God also brings sinners together and unites them in marriage, but only in His sore displeasure.) Third, you both know that you are sinful saints and that you both have your character sins, which you together will have to fight all your lives. Finally, you have learned to bring your own sins to the foot of the cross every day, and you know that you will have to go together to the cross whenever sin disturbs or disrupts the intimacy of your marriage. Never hesitate to admit when you are wrong—one of the hardest things in the world to do—and be ready always to forgive each other, even as God in Christ has forgiven you. Be sure to visit your minister, maybe even a few times, not only to discuss your wedding plans, but also to have a frank and open talk about your future and what you may expect in married life.

Above all, be sure to have your private devotions every day, presenting your concerns and your problems before the Lord and seeking His guidance as you proceed toward an entirely new phase of your life. May I suggest that you read Genesis 24, taking particular note of verse 63, which speaks of Isaac meditating in the field as he awaits the return of the servant who went to fetch him a wife from Haran. Prepare yourself for daily devotions together after you are married, for times when you can freely discuss your spiritual problems (which so many married couples ignore), as well as your physical concerns. Nothing keeps you closer together than keeping the lines of communication open with God before you are married, as well as afterward.

This is the time to make your plans for the future. You buy your furniture, you plan your home, you receive your household gifts at showers, and you make the necessary arrangements for the future. You do that together in order to learn each other's likes and dislikes and to mold your thinking into one. Particularly such questions as to which church you will belong, where is the most suitable place to live, and what sort of home best serves your purpose must be decided together, in full understanding of each other's needs.

You should also agree to have children, as many as the Lord may deem proper to entrust to you. The one serious, sinful error many young people of our day make is that they agree to practice birth control until the opportune time arrives for having children. They agree that both will work until their home is well-furnished and at least partially paid for. The mere agreement that both shall work until the first child arrives can lead to disaster. So often the wife enjoys that freedom of going out to her job, making her own money, buying luxuries she otherwise could not afford, and keeping the attachments and the friendships of the past, that she finds it extremely difficult, if not impossible, to give them up when a child in the home is long overdue.

Birth control for carnal, selfish reasons is sin. In this day when planned families are not an impossibility, we must be able to give a good account to God how we have spaced our children and why. God instituted marriage for the very purpose of having children. It is the most natural thing in the world for a husband to want a son that looks like him, or a girl that is the exact image of her mother. It is more than the natural maternal instinct of a Christian wife to want to have a baby. In a covenant home, the consideration of bringing forth covenant seed, the church of the future, far outweighs any other consideration.

If my parents had waited to have children until they could "afford" them, they would never have had any. If they had followed the modern day pattern of insisting on a small family, I would never have been born, for I was the eighth child in a busy family. Again, if in the early years of my marriage, in which the Depression of the 1930s hit us with full force, my wife and I had asked whether we could afford children, our home would have remained childless. Apart from the sin we would have committed and the lack of faith in God we would have shown, we would have missed the real joy of our married life. Children are, indeed, a heritage of the Lord, an asset that makes the home complete, an assurance that we have not lived our lives in vain, a comfort especially in old age. The lonely people, even the lonely senior citizens, are those who never had children to brighten their lives. Planning your future includes planning to have children and not postponing that until some convenient time in the future.

Finally, a word of warning. Engagement time is a time of real intimacy, as it should be. You are preparing for your own exclusive future that you hope to share together. This is the time to prove your love for each other by sexual restraint. Do not indulge in the sexual privileges that God has ordained only for the married. Do not let anyone tell you that you should experiment with sex to find out whether you are properly mated. Those who write for personal advice to Ann Landers and other newspaper columnists most often describe sexual problems that had their source in earlier sexual sins. And when does the advice they are given ever mention anything about God's will for marriage? If you love one another in the fear of the Lord, you can resist temptation, resting assured that the Lord will bind you together in holy wedlock *in His favor*, which is your only sure guarantee for a happy marriage.

Do not tempt each other beyond endurance. This is sin. When God gave us the seventh commandment, forbidding adultery and all related sins, He did not do this to lay a hard, virtually impossible burden upon us. He gave us that commandment as a rule of life, to make us happy and blessed in His fear. Also in this respect, it is joy to do His will. It really is. We bring upon ourselves untold misery, a bad conscience, distrust and suspicion, fear of the consequences, and many other griefs when we play with things holy and drag them into the cesspool of unrighteousness.

If you love each other, as you say you do, respect each other's morals, and encourage each other to resist temptation, to stand firm in the right. Keep that marriage date a day to look forward to in all the purity of the children of God. Be happy that the white gown gives expression to your faithfulness to God and to each other. Wait with patience until the Lord reveals to you that marriage is *very really* a holy institution, its bed spotless, and that even your sexual relationship in marriage is a most beautiful picture of the most intimate communion of life that we have with God in Christ Jesus. You will thank your God for years to come if you pray now for a pure heart and a pure walk together.

Chapter 6

Wedding Plans

John and Mary have set the date for their marriage, about six months away. This half year seemed to be a sensible interval, giving them ample time to make the necessary arrangements for the big event. They never realized that so much was involved in preparing for one short evening. This preparation involves trips to the photographer, to the florist, to the printer, and on and on. Dresses have to be obtained, suits ordered, colors picked out, and details attended to *ad infinitum.* The bridal party has to be planned, the ceremony arranged, the reception worked out, invitations chosen and sent . . . Will they ever get so much done in such a short time? This is all strange to John, who had never given it a thought that it took weeks of planning, shopping, and whatnot just to get married! Secretly he asks himself, "Why not just go to the minister?" For Mary this is different. I once asked a very thorough young lady at her rehearsal, "Did you start planning this already when you were twelve years old?" For an answer she gave me a big, knowing smile.

There have been some very definite improvements in our weddings and in our receptions over the years. It appears to me that getting married is taken much more seriously by our young people today than it was forty or fifty years ago. Then, weddings took place at home. All the large pieces of furniture were moved out of the living room and out of the "family room." This family room, by the way, was a sort of luxury in most homes. It had furniture, but it was not heated in the winter. In fact, it was rarely used, except for weddings and funerals and, very occasionally, for family visitation. Chairs were brought into these rooms and placed as close together as possible to accommodate all the invited guests. Usually an arch of some sort was arranged between the two rooms, where the ceremony would take place. If there was an organ in the house, someone would play an appropriate piece of music while the minister and the couple marched in. The Marriage Form was read, the couple answered their "Yes" and their "I do," followed by a prayer and the completion of the Form, and the ceremony was over.

There was something warm and intimate about this kind of ceremony, but the trouble was that when the ceremony was finished, also all the solemnity of the occasion evaporated instantly. Soon, amid a great hubbub, congratulations were extended, a lunch was served, the married couple were made the butt of a series of jokes, not always in good taste, and often a hilarious program followed. Skits and humorous dialogues were interspersed with serious poems and well-meant congratulations. Gradually, the older people decided that it was time to leave, and the evening was given over to the young people, who played games, sometimes far into the morning. I have also attended weddings in other communities that began at eleven o'clock in the morning. Lunch and supper were served to the guests that were able to spend the afternoon with the bridal couple and their families. In the evening, the young people came to have their jokes and games. In the meantime, boys and girls, and some older people of the neighborhood as well, came to chivaree, that is, to announce their arrival with shouts, beating on pots and pans, and firing gunshots into the air. They came frequently in groups, each demanding to see the bride, to share some of the food, and to receive a handout. These "fun" makers did not always leave without doing some damage to the property, to the horses and buggies, and later to the automobiles parked around the home.

There has been, however, marked improvement in our weddings throughout the years. The ceremony is far more solemn and impressive, the reception far more sober, as befits the awesomeness of the occasion. There are other improvements that can be mentioned. Our choice of music at the ceremony has improved. Songs like "O Promise Me," "Because," and the like have been replaced by songs with more spiritual content. The long familiar "Here Comes the Bride" has had its day, for which I am not sorry. Songs with real spiritual content and depth make the ceremony richer, and fit far better with the occasion. The use of renditions of the chorale-style Psalms with their dignity and deep joy is on the increase, as well as the participation of the audience with an appropriate *Psalter* number. These both add beauty, historical perspective, and spiritual depth to an occasion that should be as rich and as solemn as possible, particularly since our weddings are most often now held in the church auditorium. (The Dutch Psalms make lovely processionals and dignified recessionals, as well as song music, and there is a greater variety there than most people realize.)

Shall I tell you what I think would make an ideal wedding, both in harmony with Scripture and the Church Order, and in harmony with the significance and symbolism of marriage? A proper, Christian wedding should be a church wedding. By that I do not mean a wedding in church, but very really a church wedding. The entire congregation should be present, there should be a regular worship service with a sermon, and the wedding should be integrated into the service.

Attempts have been made in the past to have church services during the week, but these efforts have failed. The consistory was present, the entire congregation was called to worship, but only a few members of the congregation made their appearance. If the congregation is not present, the mere presence of the consistory does not make it a church wedding. Therefore, the only possibility of having a church wedding is to have the ceremony in the Sunday evening service.

Already I hear a storm of protest. First of all, would it be possible to have such a large number in the wedding party on a Sunday evening? How about the dresses of the bride and of her attendants after sitting through a service and then appearing before the whole congregation? These and other details would have to be worked out by the couple, but should hardly present insurmountable problems. I am sure that many fathers and mothers would give a sigh of relief if much of the superfluous and expensive pomp and fanfare were eliminated from our ceremony. Many others would consider it a healthy sign if the emphasis would fall upon the vows that are spoken rather than on all these distracting outward displays. I know, and I agree wholeheartedly, that this event is the big thing in the life of the bridal couple, especially of the bride. The bride has dreamed for years of this great occasion, and years later she likes to reminisce with keen delight, even telling her children what that great event meant to her. But if we learn to lay the emphasis where it belongs, our weddings will become more meaningful than they are now.

The second objection bound to come up pertains to the reception.

Having a wedding ceremony on Sunday evening would require that a large reception be held later, possibly on Monday or Tuesday evening. That also creates problems. Young people are accustomed to getting married and leaving on their honeymoon during the latter part of the week. Instead of the whole event being finished in one night, it would be spread over two nights. Instead of relatives and friends coming once, the more interested ones must come twice. This involves a bit more work, a bit more planning. Yet, as a general rule, a person gets married only once in a lifetime. This is a big, if not the biggest event in his life. The occasion is of utmost importance, both for the couples and the families involved. Those who wish to give their blessing upon the marriage will be willing to put forth a bit more effort to make this wedding the very best, as it should be.

A third objection follows out of the second. The bridal couple almost always leave on their trip immediately after the wedding. If the ceremony is held on Sunday evening, they would be compelled to stay until after the reception. But that is not all bad, either. We are such creatures of habit and custom that no one wants to break with it. I hope that sometime there will arise a couple who have the courage to be the first ones to attempt getting married on Sunday, thus breaking the ice for those who see the good of it.

A bit of serious thought will help us to realize that the advantages of a Sabbath wedding far outweigh the disadvantages. Whatever we can do to emphasize the importance of this great occasion must certainly be advantageous. A church service, with the entire congregation participating in song and in prayer, a fitting sermon that is not cut down as much as possible, would add to the spiritual benefit derived from the wedding. You and I are baptized in the church, we grow up in the church, we make our public confession of faith in the church. Later we have our children baptized in the church, and we encourage our children to put the church in the center of their lives. Why, then, should our weddings be relegated to a mere weekly occasion without the congregation present? Think about it.

That brings us back to the planning of the wedding. These plans must include some sober moments, some serious reflection. Amid all the turmoil of all the other preparations, you must realize the importance of the step you are taking. May I suggest that when you order your napkins and other printed matter, you avoid the worldly custom of mentioning the bride first? This may seem like a very small item at the moment, yet there is more involved than meets the eye. We know, as God's covenant people, that marriage is a symbol of the union of Christ and His church. You, as the bridegroom, are a picture of Christ. Would you mention Christ last? You, as the bride, are a picture of Christ's church, which he has purchased with His own blood. You want to assume your God-given place already at your wedding. Did you ever notice that in the parable of the wedding feast in Matthew 22, the cry does not arise, "Behold, the bride cometh," but "Behold, the bridegroom cometh"? Gradually but surely we have fallen into the pattern of the world by putting the bride on the foreground and virtually classifying the bridegroom as among those also present.

I spoke of moments of sober reflection. You are leaving father and mother to enter into an entirely new relationship, to establish a new home and family, to walk life's pathway together until death parts you. Yours will be an exclusive relationship, actually excluding all others. It will be the most intimate relationship conceivable, more intimate than the relationship between parents and child. Your life will be a symbol of Christ, who joins His church to Him by the mystical bond of faith, uniting us to Him in most intimate fellowship. We become flesh of His flesh, bone of His bone. We are one with Him as intimately as the head and the body are one, living one life of love and fellowship. How wonderful that our lives may be a picture of that eternal union and that our marriages may symbolize the eternal wedding feast of the Lamb! We not only *see* it, we *live* it, as in Ephesians 5:31, 32:

> For this cause shall a man leave his father and mother, and shall
> be joined unto his wife, and they two shall be one flesh. This is a
> great mystery: but I speak concerning Christ and the church.

You can best prepare yourselves by taking time to read the Marriage Form. Read it alone; read and discuss it together. Know what it teaches us, so that your wedding will be more meaningful. Take note of the fact that you are hand picked for each other by no less than God Himself. In God's eternal plan, you were His choice for each other, even as He brought you together by His providence. Notice the responsibilities that you as husband take upon yourself, and the duties that you as wife take upon yourself. Make special note of the vows you are about to take, so that when the time comes, you will be deeply aware of the promises you are making to each other before God and those present. All the excitement of the occasion must not blur from your minds the seriousness of your vows. Therefore, it is a *must* for every sincere young couple to prepare themselves individually and together in honest talks with God in prayer, open talks with both sets of parents, and sincere talks with one another. You owe it not only to yourselves, but to each other, that you are fully aware of the fact that your marriage is a holy institution of God for your happiness and blessedness, but above all, to the glory of God's Name.

Chapter 7

"And Shall Cleave unto His Wife"

"Who giveth this woman to this man?" With a practiced voice the father answers, "Her mother and I." Thereby the leaving of father and mother is complete. The father sits down with a deep awareness that the bond with the parental home is broken. The parents of the groom, as well as the bride's parents, are filled with mixed feelings. While they anticipate a vacant spot in the home, they rejoice that their child is marrying in the Lord.

Marrying in the Lord. This fact is vital: the couple eagerly steps forward to be united in the bond of holy matrimony. Already a marriage license has been obtained, signed, and sealed by the magistrate. Now the couple are ready to speak their vows to each other, vows that will bind them together as husband and wife as long as they both shall live. They are fulfilling the scriptural mandate given already in the state of perfection in paradise: "Therefore shall a man leave his father and his mother, and shall cleave unto his wife: and they shall be one flesh" (Gen. 2:24).

Why does this formality have such far-reaching implications? This question is important today, particularly because another question looms menacingly: why are two persons kept from each other, so that they may not live together sexually until the marriage vows have been spoken, and immediately afterward they are free to live together? Or still another question: why do these vows bind them so firmly and so permanently together that they may never separate, and if they would be forced to do so, it would only be by the painful and expensive formality of a legal divorce? Many would rather brush aside the marriage license and vows, live together on an experimental basis, and if the whole affair proves to be a failure, part from each other without fuss. The only reason why some women insist on a formal wedding is that they want a sense of security so that, if their marriage suffers shipwreck, they have a claim to alimony. However, obtaining a license and going through the formality of speaking vows seems too cumbersome to be of real importance to many.

A marriage license and marriage vows are intimately related. The marriage license is the legal aspect of marriage bond. The legal aspect of marriage is important. The State has something to say about marriage. This is true because marriage belongs to the creation ordinance. God instituted marriage before the fall.

This legal aspect arises out of the organic relationship of all mankind; that is, we live in this world not as individuals, but as part of the human race. John Donne wrote, "No man is an island," and this is very true. No man can take the attitude that he is responsible for his actions only to himself, as if he can do as he pleases and nobody else should care. He is a member of his family, a neighbor in his community, and a citizen of his country. As a child of God, he is a member of God's church and an integral part of the world of God's love that will be renewed in the perfection of heavenly glory.

In former times, the parents, as legal guardians, were responsible for their children marrying in a proper, legal manner. As the human race spread out, and the laws of the magistrate became more specific, the civil authorities became responsible before God for supervising the legal aspect of marriage. Therefore, the magistrate, as God's servant, has the divinely given right to demand that a marriage license be obtained and that the consent be given to a marriage in harmony with the law. For example, the civil magistrate may not grant a license to someone who is already married, since bigamy is contrary to the law of God. The law also gives consent to some responsible official—a justice of the peace, a judge, or a minister—to perform the ceremony. This official sees that the vows are properly spoken.

In The Netherlands, a double ceremony was required. A marriage was solemnized by the local magistrate and then confirmed by the church. The ceremony first took place in the city hall and then in a public worship service. Therefore, our Marriage Form has as its full title, "Form for the *Confirmation* of Marriage Before the Church." In our country, the magistrate authorizes the minister to perform the ceremony, so that the marriage is not merely "confirmed," but is actually solemnized by the minister. The entire ceremony centers about the vows that are spoken, which makes the marriage legally binding before the church and before the magistrate.

A vow, as you know, is a promise under oath. This oath-bound promise is made before God and the witnesses that are present. The vow expresses three things. First, the couple declares to each other and before all present that they are deeply aware of the presence of God. They actually call upon God to witness the promises that are made. Second, they declare that God in heaven confirms the truth and sincerity of their promises. He who searches the heart knows that they speak the truth, the whole truth, and nothing but the truth. Each makes promises to the prospective mate in sincerity of heart and mind. Third, they affirm that God, who is just, will bless them in their faithfulness to each other but will surely punish them if they transgress in any way. The common expression for this, as found in Scripture, is, "The LORD do so to me, and more also, if ought but death part thee and me" (Ruth 1:17).

This makes the marriage vow a serious matter. By this very act the bridegroom and the bride pledge fidelity to one another. The bridegroom takes his wife and promises to cleave to her as long as they shall live. The wife takes her husband and promises likewise to cleave to him and obey him as long as they shall live. Since this is done in the presence of God, it is a prayer that God may perform His mighty work now and henceforth, joining them together in one flesh, one love, and one life as long as they walk life's pathway together. It is interesting to note in this connection that the expression "to cleave" means literally "to be glued together," devotedly joined together with heart and mind with their whole being. It should also be added that whether a couple consciously makes these vows in the presence of God or makes them indifferently, God still holds them to their vows. To speak these vows lightly, carelessly, without forethought or purpose, is profanity, the sin against the third commandment. To break these vows is also serious profanity. God will *not* hold him guiltless that takes His Name in vain.

This makes the contents of the vows extremely significant. In recent years far too much emphasis falls on the external display at the ceremony, the bride and her gown, the bridal party (one seemingly trying to outdo the other with the size of the party and the magnificence of their attire), the floral arrangements, and many other additions to the ceremony. You understand, I like a nice wedding. I like to witness a ceremony that will be long remembered by the bridal couple and by others. But I bemoan the fact that far too little emphasis is placed on the heart of the matter: the vows that are spoken. It seems to have become a popular pastime for couples to change the wording of their vows, to simplify them, to put them in their own words, and often to make them meaningless. I know of no serious objection if young people prefer to memorize the vows as found in our Marriage Form and recite them to each other. But I do see serious objections if those vows are changed, so that the vows of the bride are the same as those of the groom, as if their marriage is nothing more than a fifty-fifty proposition.

The vow of the bridegroom in our Marriage Form reads as follows:

> N., do you acknowledge here, before God and this His holy church, that you have taken, and do take, to your lawful wife, N., here present, promising her never to forsake her; to love her faithfully, to maintain her, as a faithful and pious husband is bound to do to his lawful wife; that you will live holily with her; keeping faith and truth to her in all things according to the holy gospel?[1]

By this vow, the bridegroom declares publicly that he is taking his bride as his lawful wife. Two words receive the emphasis in this vow: lawful and faithful. Twice it is said that this is his lawful wife. Faithfulness is the keynote that runs through this pledge. Taking his wife involves a fourfold promise.

First, the groom promises never to forsake her. This promise is based on the scriptural teaching that the marriage bond is unbreakable. Nothing, absolutely nothing, as long as both parties are living, can break that bond. God joins together. What God joins together, man has no right to tear asunder. Often, after a few years of marriage, difficulties arise, and the complaint is readily raised, "We made a mistake. We really did not love each other after all. We were not even meant for each other." Whatever mistake the troubled couple may seem to have

---

1. *The Psalter*, 117.

made, or rather, whatever sin they made themselves guilty of, God makes no mistake when He joins two people together. Therefore, He requires this of them: "Love one another, and forgive one another, even as God in Christ has forgiven you." When the young man promises never to forsake his bride, he must realize that this is for better or for worse, for richer or for poorer, in sickness and in health, even until death breaks the earthly bond. A young man can leave father and mother to attach himself to his wife, but he cannot ever leave his wife to cling to another.

Second, the bridegroom promises that he will love his wife faithfully. As has been said before, this love is not a mere sexual urge. At the time of marriage, sexual appeal may seem to predominate. Yet married people soon learn that sexual intercourse is not an end in itself. It is the expression of the unique love whereby God unites husband and wife as one. Love between life partners is unique in every way. A man cannot love his neighbor's wife in the same way that he loves his own wife. He cannot love his sister, nor his daughter, nor, for that matter, any other person, in the manner in which he loves his wife. He sees in her an attractiveness that is only for him. She is just as appealing when he meets her across the breakfast table, or with strands of hair hanging down her face, or with clothing disheveled when she has been cleaning the house. He experiences a bond of unity in their thoughts, desires, ambitions, and aspirations. They enjoy each other's company, dreading the thought of being separated from each other, eagerly looking forward to being together again. They love each other for what they are. It has been said, "I love you not only for what *you* are, but also for what *I* am when I'm with you." Yet the strongest bond is the spiritual bond that unites them in the Lord and makes their life complete. The bridegroom promises that he will love his wife always, even in times of temptation, even when his wife is stricken with illness, physical infirmity, mental stress, or any other ailment that makes inroads into their marital relationship. The promise is not supplemented with a series of if's and but's; it is simply the promise to love his wife faithfully.

Third, the promise of the groom includes that he will "maintain" his wife, "as a faithful and pious husband is bound to do to his lawful wife." He is fully aware of his responsibility to be the head of the home that is being established. He wants to be a proper picture of Christ, who

is the head of His church (I Cor. 11:3). Our Marriage Form expresses
that rather nicely:

> You, who are the bridegroom, must know that God hath set you
> to be the head of your wife, that you, according to your ability,
> shall lead her with discretion; instructing, comforting, protecting
> her, as the head rules the body; yea, as Christ is the head, wis-
> dom, consolation, and assistance to His church. Besides you
> are to love your wife as your own body, as Christ hath loved His
> church: you shall not be bitter against her, but dwell with her as a
> man of understanding, giving honor to the wife as the weaker
> vessel, considering that ye are joint heirs of the grace of life, that
> your prayers be not hindered. And since it is God's command,
> "that the man shall eat his bread in the sweat of his face," there-
> fore you are to labor diligently and faithfully in the calling wherein
> God hath set you, that you may maintain your household hon-
> estly, and likewise have something to give to the poor.[2]

Fourth, the prospective husband promises that he "will live holily
with her; keeping faith and truth to her in all things according to the
gospel." As to their mutual relationship as husband and wife, Paul says
in I Corinthians 7:2–5,

> Nevertheless, to avoid fornication, let every man have his
> own wife, and let every woman have her own husband.
> Let the husband render unto the wife due benevolence [con-
> sideration]: and likewise also the wife unto the husband.
> The wife hath not power of her own body, but the husband:
> and likewise also the husband hath not power of his own body,
> but the wife.
> Defraud ye not one the other, except it be with consent for
> a time, that ye may give yourselves to fasting and prayer; and
> come together again, that Satan tempt you not for your inconti-
> nency.

Moreover, there must be no reason for distrust or suspicion between
the husband and wife at any time. Keeping faith means to be faithful,
worthy of trust. Keeping truth means to be open, honest with one an-

---

2. *The Psalter*, 116.

other, avoiding all personal secrets, keeping all the lines of communication open, living one life with one love, one devotion to God, and one aim: the glory of God.

The vow that is spoken by the bride is similar to the vow of the bridegroom, with the exception that it does not speak of "maintaining" him, but rather promises "to be obedient to him, to serve and assist him." That obedience is not a slavish subservience. I have known husbands, even some who professed to be serious-minded Christians, who treated their wives like slaves, ordering them about, belittling them in public, expecting them to cower and to crawl for them. That is not the love of a husband for his wife, and that kind of obedience is not required of a woman. The husband is the head of the home, and his wife is his helper, his assistant, and therefore manager of his affairs (Gen. 2:18; I Cor. 11:8, 9). The wife makes his home comfortable, pleasant, so that he can carry out his life calling with her full support. As a helper, she surrenders herself to her husband, promising henceforth to live for him. She gives up her name and assumes his name. She gives up her private ambitions to unite her aspirations with his. This is the innate nature of a woman, according to her very creation. The more a woman can live for her husband, the more she will experience the blessedness of their union in covenant life. This does not mean that she must agree with her husband when he is wrong, nor must she consent to share his sinful ambitions. She does not sell her soul when she marries, but she remains an individual confessing member of the body of Christ. In that respect there is no difference between husband and wife, no more than between bond and free, Jew or Greek, but all are one in Christ. Yet as a wife, she is bound to her lawful husband to obey him in all things right.

In a magazine article, Carolyn Lewis writes that many women picture marriage as something boring, demeaning, deadening, a form of imprisonment, and a threat to the solitary individual that imposes grueling, baffling, frustrating responsibilities on the woman. The author goes on to point out that this is not true. She says, "In our eagerness to exact equal treatment, we women seem to be forgetting who we are. We are not men. Men cannot bear children. And for a woman, the birth of a child is a transforming experience." To this the author adds,

There is nothing inconsequential or demeaning about choosing to make a child one's life work. Nor is there anything shameful in wanting to make life comfortable and happy for another adult human, like a husband. There are good and useful and important things to do inside the home, and the woman's movement makes light of that fact at its peril.[3]

A believing wife has so much more reason to realize how important her life is when she obeys, serves, and assists her husband in serving the Lord. For her, it is a privilege to have children, for she is "saved in childbearing." Scripture points out to us that sin came into the world by the woman, yet God has privileged the woman to bring forth the covenant seed, the church (I Tim. 2:13–15). Throughout the ages, believing women (Hannah, Elisabeth, Mary, to mention a few) have considered themselves blessed in bringing forth the covenant seed. The church throughout the ages has sung from the heart:

In thy wife thou shalt have gladness,
    She shall fill thy home with good,
Happy in her loving service
    And the joys of motherhood.[4]

It is after the marriage vows are spoken that one man and one woman are declared husband and wife, and they become one flesh. Not the minister, not a justice of the peace, but God in heaven joins these two lives together into one. The legal aspect of the marriage bond is established. The physical, psychological, and spiritual strands continue to join in perfect unity until, as often happens, an elderly couple even look very much alike. The newlyweds do well to lift up their hearts in prayer to God, asking for His continued blessing that in their lives they may be an earthly picture of Christ and His church.

---

3. Carolyn Lewis, "A Different Sort of Liberation," *Reader's Digest,* 112 (March 1978), 117, 118.
4. *The Psalter,* Psalter No. 360.

Chapter 8

"And They Shall Be One Flesh"

John and Mary have now left father and mother and are experiencing the merging process of married life. Their life together is far different from what they had anticipated. It is far more wonderful, far happier, but also a bit more difficult than they had realized. They are always together now under the same roof, except for short breaks in the day. They make their plans together, go to church together, have their family worship together. They no more go their way as individuals, but share their lives. This new togetherness demands agreement, understanding, consideration, cooperation; it demands a love that they can share only as "one flesh."

We have had opportunity in the previous chapters to speak of the physical and psychological strands that unite two persons in marital union. We have also spoken of the legal aspect of the marriage bond, whereby God cements them together under the solemn declaration, "What therefore God hath joined together, let not man put asunder." There is a third bond, actually the most important of all for a happy marriage, and that is the spiritual bond that unites the children of God in the Lord. The expression "one flesh" does not refer merely to a physical union, nor even only to a physical-psychical union, but to a complete union of body, soul, and spirit. The couple is married, first of all, to God, and thus spiritually to each other. It is this spiritual bond that makes it possible to speak of the *holy marriage state* in a world of sin.

No one dare question the fact that marriage was holy as it was instituted by God in paradise. Adam was formed by the Creator from the dust of the earth as a male; Eve was taken from Adam's rib as a female. Adam had a strong, manly body and a large, dexterous hand capable of hard work. His facial features were masculine. Psychologically he thought, reasoned, desired, and planned as a man. Even as the image bearer of God, created in God's image and likeness to know, to love, and to serve His God, he was entirely masculine. His whole makeup fitted him to father children and to be a father for them. On the other hand, Eve's body, her long flowing hair, and her facial features were those of a woman. Psychologically she was a woman. Spiritually, as a friend-servant of God, she was completely female. By God's creation ordinance Adam was head of the woman and father of the human race; Eve was his helper and the mother of all mankind. No one and nothing can change this creation ordinance of God; do what he will in defiance of God's laws, man can never be anything but a male; the woman can never be anything but a female. Eve was exactly what Adam needed to make his life complete in paradise. He needed a companion with whom he could communicate. We can understand that. Adam needed the companionship of sharing. He could not evaluate or enjoy his deepest feelings without communing with the woman as his touchstone. Adam enjoyed the intimate fellowship that he experienced with Eve in the garden.

Without Eve, Adam could never have been the organic and representative head of the human race. Adam was capable of fathering a child, but it is the woman's unique distinction that only she can give birth to the child. Already in the state of righteousness our parents were aware of this, but even more so after the fall when they awaited the Savior, who would be born of a woman.

Finally, the marital relationship between Adam and Eve was a picture of their intimate union with God in Christ. They were privileged to experience God's covenant fellowship in their own intimate relationship. Scripture speaks of the covenant union between God and His church as a marriage, pointing us to God's eternal faithfulness and unchanging love. In the prophecy of Isaiah, for example, God asks Israel in captivity to produce, if they can, a bill of divorcement whereby He sent them away. Although they were temporarily banished from His land because of their spiritual adultery, God never ceased loving them, never cast them away completely with a divorce, but drew His unfaithful wife back to Him with the power of His undying love. In the prophecy of Hosea, there is also repeated reference to the marriage relationship between God and His church in Christ. In the New Testament Jesus speaks of the wedding feast of the King's Son, and the book of Revelation tells of the culmination of Christ's union with His church in that day when He takes His bride into the wedding chamber to celebrate with her the wedding feast of eternal, covenant life and blessedness in the new creation. The most intimate relationship between one man and one woman is an exclusive relationship, barring all others, yet at the same time an all-inclusive relationship of love and devotion, the like of which there is none other on earth, as a reflection of our communion of life with the living God. In a sense, husband and wife not only reflect that communion of life with God, but they also live it in their own close oneness of heart and mind, of soul and body, in their daily relationship with one another.

It is true that this holy marriage state as it was instituted in paradise was corrupted by sin. In fact, the marital relationship between Adam and Eve was the first to suffer. Eve must have forgotten her subjection to her husband, for she felt quite confident that she could carry on the conversation with Satan alone, even when that conversation turned toward the forbidden tree. Although she soon realized that she was getting involved in some serious problems, she failed to retrace her steps. She knew that she was not taking seriously the warning of God when she told Satan that they might die if they ate of the forbidden fruit. Eve must have felt the sting of Satan's lie when he contradicted God with his defiant, "Ye shall not surely die." She knew very well that Adam would not allow such blasphemy. Independently she decided that she could eat of the forbidden tree and escape the consequences. It even appealed to her to satisfy this newly aroused craving for that forbidden fruit, especially because she hoped that Satan might be right in proposing that she would become independent, to do as she wished, even as God. Without any further thought about consulting Adam, she reached out and ate.

It was only after she had fallen that she realized what a serious breach she had made in their marriage. She was no longer holy; her marriage was no longer holy. Adam could no longer love her, since she had broken the covenant with God and allied herself with Satan against

God. She realized that she did not love Adam any more as before, since he was righteous and could only condemn her for her indiscretion and sin. What was still worse, Adam's helper became his adversary. Cunningly she devised, under the instigation of the devil, ways and means to lure her husband into the same evil into which she had fallen. And she succeeded.

The deed was no sooner done than Adam and Eve looked at each other with entirely different eyes. They were no longer motivated by a holy love. Unholy, sexual lust flooded their souls, so that they both rushed off to find cover, devising fig leaves as an improvised cloak for their sin. No wonder that Adam and Eve fled from before the sight of God, who could no longer justly be their Friend-Sovereign. Vainly Adam brought up the lame excuse, "The woman whom thou gavest to be with me, she gave me of the tree, and I did eat." This was true all right, but it was a strong evidence of the breach that had come between them. Not only their holy love was corrupted, but their perfect harmony was also disrupted. The breach of sin yawned like a great gap between them. Irremediable scars remained. The damage would never be completely undone. Their marriage had suffered disaster.

God came to them, not with the rumblings of the thunder of judgment, as at Sinai, but with the call of grace, calling them unto Himself. God came in Christ, as the only One who is able to keep covenant forever. God took them by the hands, as it were, and led them as repentant sinners to the cross of Jesus, where they met each other face to face, confessed their sin to God and to each other, and found mercy. In Christ their marriage was once more restored as a holy state, rooted in the eternal love of God who keeps covenant forever. The spiritual bond was restored in Christ, even in a richer sense than they could have experienced in paradise. This same spiritual bond unites all true children of God in the Lord.

This does not mean that there is no real marriage among sinners in the world. Although the spiritual bond is lacking, the physical and psychological bonds, as well as the legal aspect of marriage, still remain. Our Canons speak of "glimmerings of natural light," even after the fall:

> There remain, however, in man since the fall, the glimmerings of

natural light, whereby he retains some knowledge of God, of natural things, and of the differences between good and evil, and discovers some regard for virtue, good order in society, and for maintaining an orderly external deportment.[1]

This article of the Canons goes on to say that man renders the natural light wholly polluted, and holds it in unrighteousness, so that he is inexcusable before God. However, the sinner does possess sufficient natural light that he can live in the intimate union of husband and wife, and even desires such a union.

The point I want to make is that the creation ordinance continues, so that marriage as an institution of God is still in force. Therefore, amid all the sexual corruption, immorality both within and outside marriage, abortions, divorces, and remarriages, there is still a possibility for a decent and comparatively "happy" marriage in the world. Many married people do live together all their lives. Many husbands are good to their wives, knowing that gentleness and understanding are to their own advantage. Many wives do respect their husbands, care for their needs, and are content to provide a home for their family. Married couples may be highly respected in their community. *But* the one essential ingredient for a truly happy marriage is lacking: the spiritual bond that unites two hearts in Christ. The grace of God does not rest on that home. An unbelieving couple that gains the whole world, yet loses their souls, ends up in hell. The husband will not thank his wife for being a good wife, the wife will not thank her husband for being a good provider, nor will the children thank their parents for having brought them to that horrible place of torment. The curse of the Lord rests upon the mansion of the ungodly rich; His blessing abides in the tent of the godly poor.

May this be a warning to anyone who contemplates a mixed marriage, that is, one who is thinking of marrying an unbeliever or a person of contrary convictions. A lifetime is a long time to repent of the foolishness of youth.

In the world, sex is a dirty word. Most people cannot hear or use the

---

1. Canons of Dordrecht, Heads III & IV, Article 4.

word without lustful thoughts and desires flooding the soul. Some minds are so filthy that their conversation is saturated with vile and suggestive expressions. There was a time when the word "sex" was taboo, even considered an improper word to be spoken aloud. Sexual intercourse between married people was referred to with a hand hiding the mouth. Women were embarrassed to admit that they were pregnant, and they went into hiding during the last weeks of their pregnancy. All this has changed, in a sense for the better. Children need no longer learn about sex in back alleys and from smutty novels secreted into the bedroom. Yet there is a danger that the pendulum has swung too far in the opposite direction, where the private life of the wedded pair is paraded before the public. The completely exclusive, yet at the same time the completely inclusive union of married couples is experienced only in the realm of grace.

The believing husband readily accepts his position as provider for his wife and family, conscious of the fact that God is their great Provider. The wife assumes her position as subject to her husband in all things, even as the church is subject to Christ. She considers his wants and needs as a faithful wife in obedience to her husband. Love does not demand, but gives. Love is not selfish, but is kind, considerate, devoted. Although both the husband and the wife see each other's faults and weaknesses better than anyone else sees them, although they often must bear with one another, often must meet at the cross to forgive each other, yet the bond of love that unites them in the Lord binds their hearts and souls together in a growing need for each other. This has a sanctifying influence on their outlook on life and on their regard for each other. Dreams of an expensive home, new cars, trips and vacations at regular intervals, campers, boats, and other luxuries become secondary in their lives. The husband loves his wife as his own body, so that, if need be, he would die for her. The wife realizes that her husband's life is her life, his calling is her calling, his concerns are her concerns, his welfare and peace of mind are her contentment. Even as he would die for her, so she would live solely for him. Their life is a giving to each other, even as God gives Himself to us, to the extent that He brings us into His very heart, into His fellowship, into the intimate communion of life with Him, reflecting His glory.

In a holy marriage state, also the sexual relationship of husband and wife is sanctified in the Lord. The new life in Christ, at least in principle, governs both soul and body. Husband and wife are not drawn to each other merely to satisfy their sexual urge, but by the strong bond of unique love that unites them as one flesh. They admire one another; they esteem one another; they need, long for, even desire one another as two individuals who are especially adapted to each other. They express to each other their mutual devotion, their oneness of soul and body, of mind and will, of fellowship and life. This complete surrender to each other with body and soul is at the same time an expression of their spiritual unity. They open their souls to each other unashamed, for they love, they seek, they need, they find each other as husband and wife in the Lord. From that aspect their intercourse is not sinful, but an expression of their holy union in Christ. Their love is rooted in Christ's love for His church, His bride, even as they so richly experience that love in their own lives. In the deepest sense husband and wife say to each other, "I love you, because you and I love the Lord." Their intimacy reflects the bond of intimate fellowship between Christ and them by the bond of faith that unites them together and that comes to expression in their mutual prayer-life. Their need for each other reflects the need of Christ for His own, and the need of that people for Him. Their longing reflects the longing of the Bridegroom for His bride, and of the bride for the Bridegroom, a longing that will be satisfied only within the hall of the wedding feast of the Lamb. Their comfort in each other stems from the great Comforter, the Holy Spirit, who dwells within them. Marriage in its spiritual reality is living the love of God, experiencing His covenant faithfulness and abiding love, enjoying a small foretaste of the blessedness of the life to come. Only two hearts that are spiritually united in Christ can understand that blessedness, even as it grows throughout the years of holy marital union.

What is even more amazing than that is the fact that God uses the sexual union of husband and wife to bring forth the covenant seed, the church of tomorrow. Covenant parents want children, not to satisfy their personal pride or whims, but in order to serve unto the gathering of God's church and the coming of His kingdom. They also want to experience in their own lives the grace of God that makes them heirs of salvation, even in their generations, as God repeatedly said when he promised that He would forever be the God of His people and their seed (as in Gen. 17:7). They cherish the day when they can stand together at baptism before God and His church, promising to bring up the child or children entrusted to them in the fear of the Lord to the utmost of their power. And they await the day when they stand together before the great white throne to declare, "See us, Lord, and the children Thou hast given us. *For we are Thine!*"

In anticipation, the church of all ages sings,

> Blest the man that fears Jehovah,
>   Walking ever in His ways;
> By thy toil thou shalt be prospered
>   And be happy all thy days.
>
> In thy wife thou shalt have gladness,
>   She shall fill thy home with good,
> Happy in her loving service
>   And the joys of motherhood.[2]

---

2. *The Psalter,* Psalter No. 360.